The Instructions of Commodianus

The Instructions of Commodianus

The Instructions of Commodianus

© Lighthouse Publishing 2018

All rights reserved. Without limiting the rights under copyright reserved above, no part of this publication may be reproduced, stored in a retrieval system, or transmitted, in any form or by any means (electronic, mechanical, photocopying, recording or otherwise), without the prior written permission of the copyright owner of this book.

Published by
Lighthouse Christian Publishing
SAN 257-4330
5531 Dufferin Drive
Savage, Minnesota, 55378
United States of America

www.lighthousechristianpublishing.com

The Instructions of Commodianus

Introductory Note.

[a.d. 240.] Our author seems to have been a North-African bishop, of whom little is known save what we learn from his own writings. He has been supposed to incline to some ideas of Praxeas, and also to the Millenarians, but perhaps on insufficient grounds. His Millenarianism reflects the views of a very primitive age, and that without the corrupt Chiliasm of a later period, which brought about a practical repudiation of the whole system. Of his writings, two poems only remain, and of these the second, a very recent discovery, has no place in the Edinburgh series. I greatly regret that it cannot be included in ours.

As a poetical work the following prose version probably does it no injustice. His versification is pronounced very crabbed, and his diction is the wretched *patois* of North Africa. But the piety and earnestness of a practical Christian seem everywhere conspicuous in this fragment of antiquity.

The Instructions of Commodianus in favor of Christian Discipline,

Against the Gods of the Heathens.

(Expressed in Acrostics.)

I.—Preface.

My preface sets forth the way to the wanderer and a good visitation when the goal of life shall have come, that he may become eternal—a thing which ignorant hearts disbelieve. I in like manner have wandered for a long time, by giving attendance upon *heathen* fanes, my parents themselves being ignorant. Thence at length I withdrew myself by reading concerning the law. I bear witness to the Lord; I grieve alas, the crowd of citizens! Ignorant of what it loses in going to seek vain gods. Thoroughly taught by these things, I instruct the ignorant in the truth.

II.—God's Indignation.

In the law, the Lord of heaven, and earth, and sea has commanded, saying, Worship not vain gods made by your own hands out of wood or gold, lest my wrath destroy you for such things. The people before Moses, unskilled, abiding without law, and ignorant of God, prayed to gods that perished, after the likenesses of which they fashioned vain idols. The Lord having brought the Jews out of the land of Egypt, subsequently imposed on them a law; and the Omnipotent enjoined these things, that they should serve Him alone, and not those idols. Moreover, in that law is taught concerning the resurrection, and the hope of living in happiness again in the world, if vain idols be forsaken and not worshipped.

III.—The Worship of Demons.

When Almighty God, to beautify the nature of the world, willed that that earth should be visited by angels, when they were sent down they despised His laws. Such was the beauty of women, that it turned them aside; so that, being contaminated, they could not return to heaven. Rebels from God, they uttered words against Him. Then the Highest uttered His judgment against them; and from their seed giants are said to have been born. By them arts were made known in the earth, and they taught the dyeing of wool, and everything which is done; and to them, when they died, men erected images. But the Almighty, because they were of an evil seed, did not approve that, when dead, they should be brought back from death. Whence wandering they now subvert many bodies, and it is such as these especially that ye this day worship and pray to as gods.

IV.—Saturn.

And Saturn the old, if he is a god, how does he grow old? Or if he was a god, why was he driven by his terrors to devour his children? But because he was not a god, he consumed the bowels of his sons in a monstrous madness. He was a king upon earth, born in the Mount Olympus; and he was not divine, but called himself a god. He fell into weakness of mind, and swallowed a stone for his son. Thus he became a god; of late he is called Jupiter.

V.—Jupiter.

This Jupiter was born to Saturn in the island of Breta; and when he was grown up, he deprived his father of the kingdom. He then deluded the wives and sisters of the nobles. Moreover, Pyracmon, a smith, had made for him a scepter. In the beginning God made the heaven, the earth, and the sea. But that frightful creature, born in the midst of time, went forth as a youth from a cave, and was nourished by stealth. Behold, that God is the author of all things, not that Jupiter.

VI.—Of the Same Jupiter's Thunderbolt.

Ye say, O fools, Jupiter thunders. It is he that hurls thunderbolts; and if it was childishness that thought thus, why for two hundred years have ye been babies? And will ye still be so always? Infancy is passed into maturity, old age does not enjoy trifles, the age of boyhood has departed; let the mind of youth in like manner depart. Your thoughts ought to belong to the character of men. Thou art then a fool, to believe that it is Jupiter that thunders. He, born on the earth, is nourished with goats' milk. Therefore, if Saturn had devoured him, who was it in those times that sent rain when he was dead? Especially, if a god may be thought to be born of a mortal father, Saturn grew old on the earth, and on the earth he died. There was none that predicted his previous birth. Or if he thunders, the law would have been given by him. The stories that the poets feign seduce you. He, however, reigned in Crete, and there died. He who to you is the Almighty became Alcmena's lover; he himself would in like manner be in love with living men now if he were alive. Ye pray to unclean gods, and ye call them heavenly who are born of mortal seed from those giants. Ye hear and ye read that he was born in the earth: whence was it that that corrupter so well deserved to ascend into heaven? And the Cyclopes are said to have forged him a thunderbolt; for though he was immortal, he received arms from mortals. Ye have conveyed to heaven by your authority one guilty of so many crimes, and, moreover, a parricide of his own relations.

VII.—Of the Septizonium and the Stars.

Your want of intelligence deceives you concerning the circle of the zone, and perchance from that you find out that you must pray to Jupiter. Saturn is told of there, but it is as a star, for he was driven forth by Jupiter, or let Jupiter be believed to be in the star. He who controlled the constellations of the pole, and the sower of the soil; he who made war with the Trojans, he loved the beautiful Venus. Or among the stars themselves Mars was caught with her by married jealousy: he is called the youthful god. Oh excessively foolish, to think that those who are born of Maia rule from the stars, or that they rule the entire nature of the world! Subjected to wounds, and themselves living under the dominion of the fates, obscene, inquisitive, warriors of an impious life; and they made sons, equally mortal with themselves, and were all terrible, foolish, strong, in the sevenfold girdle. If ye worship the stars, worship also the twelve signs *of the zodiac*, as well the ram, the bull, the twins, as the fierce lion; and finally, they go on into fishes, — cook them and you will prove them. A law without law is your refuge: what wishes to be, will prevail. A woman desires to be wanton; she seeks to live without restraint. Ye yourselves will be what ye wish for, and pray to as gods and goddesses. Thus I worshipped while I went astray, and now I condemn it.

VIII.—Of the Sun and Moon.

Concerning the Sun and Moon ye are in error, although they are in our immediate presence; in that ye, as I formerly did, think that you must pray to them. They, indeed, are among the stars; but they do not run of their own accord. The Omnipotent, when He established all things at first, placed them there with the stars, on the fourth day. And, indeed,

He commanded in the law that none should worship them. Ye worship so many gods who promise nothing concerning life, whose law is not on the earth, nor are they themselves foretold. But a few priests seduce you, who say that any deity destined to die can be of service. Draw near now, read, and learn the truth.

IX.—Mercury.

Let your Mercury be depicted with a Saraballum, and with wings on his helmet or his cap, and in other respects naked. I see a marvelous thing, a god flying with a little satchel. Run, poor creatures, with your lap spread open when he flies, that he may empty his satchel: do ye from thence be prepared. Look on the painted one, since he will thus cast you money from on high: then dance ye securely. Vain man, art thou not mad, to worship painted gods in heaven? If thou knowest not how to live, continue to dwell with the beasts.

X.—Neptune.

Ye make Neptune a god descended from Saturn; and he wields a trident that he may spear the fishes. It is plain by his being thus provided that he is a sea-god. Did not he himself with Apollo raise up walls for the Trojans? How did that poor stone-mason become a god? Did not he beget the cyclops-monster? And was he himself when dead unable to live again, though his structure admitted of this? Thus begotten, he begot who was already once dead.

XI.—Apollo the Soothsaying and False.

Ye make Apollo a player on the cithara, and divine. Born at first of Maia, in the isle of Delos, subsequently, for offered wages, a builder, obeying the king Laomedon, he reared the walls of the Trojans. And he established himself, and ye are seduced into thinking him a god, in whose bones the love of Cassandra burned, whom the virgin craftily sported with, and, though a divine being, he is deceived. By his office of augur he was able to know the double-hearted one. Moreover, rejected, he, though divine, departed thence. Him the virgin burnt up with her beauty, whom he ought to have burnt up; while she ought first of all to have loved the god who thus lustfully began to love Daphne, and still follows her up, wishing to violate the maid. The fool loves in vain. Nor can he obtain her by running. Surely, if he were a god, he would come up with her through the air. She first came under the roof, and the divine being remained outside. The race of men deceive you, for they were of a sad way of life. Moreover, he is said to have fed the cattle of Admetus. While in imposed sports he threw the quoit into the air, he could not restrain it as it fell, and it killed his friend. That was the last day of his companion Hyacinthus. Had he been divine, he would have foreknown the death of his friend.

XII.—Father Liber—Bacchus.

Ye yourselves say that Father Liber was assuredly twice begotten. First of all, he was born in India of Proserpine and Jupiter, and waging war against the Titans, when his blood was shed, he expired even as one of mortal men. Again, restored from his death, in another womb Semele conceived him again of Jupiter, a second Maia, whose womb being divided, he is taken away near to birth from his dead mother, and as a nursling is given to be nourished to Nisus. From this being twice born he is called Dionysus; and his religion is falsely observed in vanity; and they celebrate his orgies such that now they themselves seem to be either foolhardy or burlesquers of Mimnermomerus. They conspire in evil; they practice beforehand with pretended heat, that they may deceive others into saying that a deity is present. Hence you manifestly see men living a life like his, violently excited with the wine which he himself had pressed out; they have given him divine honor in the midst of their drunken excess.

XIII.—The Unconquered One.

The unconquered one was born from a rock, if he is regarded as a god. Now tell us, then, on the other hand, which is the first of these two. The rock has overcome the god: then the creator of the rock has to be sought after. Moreover, you still depict him also as a thief; although, if he were a god, he certainly did not live by theft. Assuredly he was of earth, and of a monstrous nature. And he turned other people's oxen into his caves; just as did Cacus, that son of Vulcan.

XIV.—Sylvanus.

Whence, again, has Sylvanus appeared to be a god? Perhaps it is agreeable *so to call him* from this, that the pipe sings sweetly because he bestows the wood; for, perhaps, it might not be so. Thou hast bought a venal master, when thou shalt have bought from him. Behold the wood fails! What is due to him? Art thou not ashamed, O fool, to adore such pictures? Seek one God who will allow you to live after death. Depart from such as have become dead in life.

XV.—Hercules.

Hercules, because he destroyed the monster of the Aventine Mount, who had been wont to steal the herds of Evander, *is a god*: the rustic mind of men, untaught also, when they wished to return thanks instead of praise to the absent thunderer, senselessly vowed victims as to a god to be besought, they made milky altars as a memorial to themselves. Thence it arises that he is worshipped in the ancient manner. But he is no god, although he was strong in arms.

XVI.—Of the Gods and Goddesses.

Ye say that they are gods who are plainly cruel, and ye say that genesis assigns the fates to you. Now, then, say to whom first of all sacred rites are paid. Between the ways on either side immature death is straying. If the fates give the generations, why do you pray to the god? Thou art vainly deceived who art seeking to beseech the manes, and thou namest them to be lords over thee who are fabricated. Or, moreover, I know not what women you pray to as goddesses— Bellona and Nemesis the goddesses, together with the celestial Fury, the Virgins and Venus, for whom your wives are weak in the loins. Besides, there are in the lanes other demons which are not as yet numbered, and are worn on the neck, so that they themselves cannot give to themselves an account. Plagues ought rather to be exported to the ends of the earth.

XVII.—Of Their Images.

A few wicked and empty poets delude you; while they seek with difficulty to procure their living, they adorn falsehood to be for others under the guise of mystery. Thence feigning to be smitten by some deity, they sing of his majesty, and weary themselves under his form. Ye have often seen the Dindymarii, with what a din they enter upon luxuries while they seek to feign the furies, or when they strike their backs with the filthy axe, although with their teaching they keep what they heal by their blood. Behold in what name they do not compel those who first of all unite themselves to them with a sound mind. But that they may take away a gift, they seek such minds. Thence see how all things are feigned. They cast a shadow over a simple people, lest they should believe, while they perish, the thing once for all proceeded in vanity from antiquity, that a prophet who uttered false things might be believed; but their majesty has spoken naught.

The Instructions of Commodianus

XVIII.—Of Ammydates and the Great God.

We have already said many things of an abominable superstition, and yet we follow up the subject, lest we should be said to have passed anything over. And the worshippers worshipped their Ammydates after their manner. He was great to them when there was gold in the temple. They placed their heads under his power, as if he were present. It came to the highest point that Cæsar took away the gold. The deity failed, or fled, or passed away into fire. The author of this wickedness is manifest who formed this same god, and falsely prophesying seduces so many and so great men, and only was silent about Him who was accustomed to be divine. For voices broke forth, as if with a changed mind, as if the wooden god were speaking into his ear. Say now yourselves if they are not false deities? From that prodigy how many has that prophet destroyed? He forgot to prophesy who before was accustomed to prophesy; so those prodigies are feigned among those who are greedy of wine, whose damnable audacity feigns deities, for they were carried about, and such an image was dried up. For both he himself is silent, and no one prophesies concerning him at all. But ye wish to ruin yourselves.

XIX.—Of the Vain Nemesiaci.

Is it not ignominy, that a prudent man should be seduced and worship such a one, or say that a log is Diana? You trust a man who in the morning is drunk, costive, and ready to perish, who by art speaks falsely what is seen by him. While he lives strictly, he feeds on his own bowels. A detestable one defiles all the citizens; and he has attached to himself—a similar gathering being made—those with whom he feigns the history, that he may adorn a god. He is ignorant how to prophesy for himself; for others he dares it. He places it on his shoulder when he pleases, and again he places it down. Whirling round, he is turned by himself with the tree of the two-forked one, as if you would think that he was inspired with the deity of the wood. Ye do not worship the gods whom they themselves falsely announce; ye worship the priests themselves, fearing them vainly. But if thou art strong in heart, flee at once from the shrines of death.

XX.—The Titans.

Ye say that the Titans are to you *Tutans*. Ye ask that these fierce ones should be silent under your roof, as so many Lares, shrines, images made like to a Titan. For ye foolishly adore those who have died by an evil death, not reading their own law. They themselves speak not, and ye dare to call them gods who are melted out of a brazen vessel; ye should rather melt them into little vessels for yourselves.

XXI.—The Montesiani.

Ye call the mountains also gods. Let them rule in gold, darkened by evil, and aiding with an averted mind. For if a pure spirit and a serene mind remained to you, thou thyself ought to examine for thyself concerning them. Thou art become senseless as a man, if thou thinkest that these can save thee, whether they rule or whether they cease. If thou seekest anything healthy, seek rather the righteousness of the law, that brings the help of salvation, and says that you are becoming eternal. For what you shall follow in vanity rejoices you for a time. Thou art glad for a brief space, and afterwards bewailest in the depths. Withdraw thyself from these, if thou wilt rise again with Christ.

XXII.—The Dullness of the Age.

Alas, I grieve, citizens, that ye are thus blinded by the world. One runs to the lot; another gazes on the birds; another, having shed the blood of bleating animals, calls forth the manes, and credulously desires to hear vain responses. When so many leaders and kings have taken counsel concerning life, what benefit has it been to them to have known even its portents? Learn, I beg you, citizens, what is good; beware of idol-fanes. Seek, indeed, all of you, in the law of the Omnipotent. Thus it has pleased the Lord of lords Himself in the heavens, that demons should wander in the world for our discipline. And yet, on the other hand, He has sent out His mandates, that they who forsake their altars shall become inhabitants of heaven. Whence I am not careful to argue this in a small treatise. The law teaches; it calls on you in your midst. Consider for yourselves. Ye have entered upon two roads; decide upon the right one.

XXIII.—Of Those Who are Everywhere Ready.

While thou obeyest the belly, thou sayest that thou art innocent; and, as if courteously, makest thyself everywhere ready. Woe to thee, foolish man! thou thyself lookest around upon death. Thou seekest in a barbarous fashion to live without law. Thou thyself hymnist thyself also to play upon a word, who feignest thyself simple. I live in simplicity with such
a one. Thou believest that thou livest, whilst thou desirest to fill thy belly. To sit down disgracefully of no account in thy house, ready for feasting, and to run away from precepts. Or because thou believest not that God will judge the dead, thou foolishly makest thyself ruler of heaven instead of Him. Thou regardest thy belly as if thou canst provide for it. Thou seemest at one time to be profane, at another to be holy. Thou appearest as a suppliant of God, under the aspect of a tyrant. Thou shalt feel in thy fates by whose law thou art aided.

XXIV.—Of Those Who Live Between the Two.

Thou who thinkest that, by living doubtfully between the two, thou art on thy guard, goest on thy way stript of law, broken down by luxury. Thou art looking forward vainly to so many things, why seekest thou unjust things? And whatever thou hast done shall there remain to thee when dead. Consider, thou foolish one, thou wast not, and lo, thou art seen. Thou knowest not whence thou hast proceeded, nor whence thou art nourished. Thou avoidest the excellent and benignant God of thy life, and thy Governor, who would rather wish thee to live. Thou turnest thyself to thyself, and givest thy back to God. Thou drownest thyself in darkness, whilst thou thinkest thou art abiding in light. Why runnest thou in the synagogue to the Pharisees, that He may become merciful to thee, whom thou of thy own accord deniest? Thence thou goest abroad again; thou seekest healthful things. Thou wishest to live between both ways, but thence thou shalt perish. And, moreover, thou sayest, Who is He who has redeemed from death, that we may believe in Him, since there punishments are awarded? Ah! not thus, O malignant man, shall it be as thou thinkest. For to him who has lived well there is advantage after death. Thou, however, when one day thou diest, shalt be taken away in an evil place. But they who believe in Christ shall be led into a good place, and those to whom that delight is given are caressed; but to you who are of a double mind, against you is punishment without the body. The course of the tormentor stirs you up to cry out against your brother.

XXV.—They Who Fear and Will Not Believe.

How long, O foolish man, wilt thou not acknowledge Christ? Thou avoidest the fertile field, and castest thy seeds on the sterile one. Thou seekest to abide in the wood where the thief is delaying. Thou sayest, I also am of God; and thou wanderest out of doors. Now at length, after so many

invitations, enter within the palace. Now is the harvest ripe, and the time so many times prepared. Lo, now reap! What! dost thou not repent? Thence now, if thou hast not, gather the seasonable wines. The time of believing to life is present in the time of death. The first law of God is the foundation of the subsequent law. Thee, indeed, it assigned to believe in the second law. Nor are threats from Himself, but from it, powerful over thee. Now astounded, swear that thou wilt believe in Christ; for the Old Testament proclaims concerning Him. For it is needful only to believe in Him who was dead, to be able to rise again to live for all time. Therefore, if thou art one who disbelievest that these things shall be, at length he shall be overcome in his guilt in the second death. I will declare
things to come in few words in this little treatise. In it can be known when hope must be preferred. Still I exhort you as quickly as possible to believe in Christ.

XXVI.—To Those Who Resist the Law of Christ the Living God.

Thou rejectest, unhappy one, the advantage of heavenly discipline, and rushest into death while wishing to stray without a bridle. Luxury and the short-lived joys of the world are ruining thee, whence thou shalt be tormented in hell for all time. They are vain joys with which thou art foolishly delighted. Do not these make thee to be a man dead? Cannot
thirty years at length make thee a wise man? Ignorant how thou hast first strayed, look upon ancient time, thou thinkest now to enjoy here a joyous life in the midst of wrongs. These are the ruins of thy friends, wars, or wicked frauds, thefts with bloodshed: the body is vexed with sores, and groaning and wailing is indulged; whether a slight disease invade thee, or thou art held down by long sickness, or thou art bereaved of thy children, or thou mournest over a lost wife. All is a wilderness: alas, dignities are hurried down from their height by vices and poverty; doubly so, assuredly, if thou languishest long. And

callest thou it life when this life of glass is mortal? Consider now at length that this time is of no avail, but in the future you have hope without the craft of living. Certainly the little children which have been snatched away desired to live. Moreover, the young men who have been deprived of life, perchance were preparing to grow old, and they themselves were making ready to enjoy joyful days; and yet we unwillingly lay aside all things in the world. I have
delayed with a perverse mind, and I have thought that the life of this world was a true one; and I judged that death would come in like manner as ye did—that when once life had departed, the soul also was dead and perished. These things, however, are not so; but the Founder and Author of the world has certainly required the brother slain by a brother. Impious man, say, said He, where is thy brother? and he denied. For the blood of thy brother has cried aloud to Me to heaven. Thou art tormented, I see, when thou thoughtest to feel nothing; but he lives and occupies the place on the right hand. He enjoys delights which thou, O wicked one, hast lost; and when thou hast called back the world, he also has gone before, and will be immortal: for thou shalt wail in hell. Certainly God lives, who makes the dead to live, that He may give worthy rewards to the innocent and to the good; but to the fierce and impious, cruel hell. Commence, O thou who art led away, to perceive
the judgments of God.

XXVII.—O Fool, Thou Dost Not Die to God.

O fool, thou dost not absolutely die; nor, when dead, dost thou escape the lofty One. Although thou shouldst arrange that when dead thou perceivest nothing, thou shalt foolishly
be overcome. God the Creator of the world liveth, whose laws cry out that the dead are in existence. But thou, whilst recklessly thou seekest to live without God, judgest that in death is extinction, and thinkest that it is absolute. God has not

ordered it as thou thinkest, that the dead are forgetful of what they have previously done. Now has the governor made for us receptacles of death, and after our ashes we shall behold them. Thou art stripped, O foolish one, who thinkest that by death thou art not, and hast made thy Ruler and Lord to be able to do nothing. But death is not a mere vacuity, if thou reconsiderest in thine heart. Thou mayest know that He is to be desired, for late thou shalt perceive Him. Thou wast the ruler of the flesh; certainly flesh ruled not thee. Freed from it, the former is buried; thou art here. Rightly is mortal man separated from the flesh. Therefore, mortal eyes will not be able to be equaled (to divine things). Thus our depth keeps us from the secret of God. Give thou now, whilst in weakness thou art dying, the honor to God, and believe that Christ will bring thee back living from the dead. Thou oughtest to give praises in the church to the omnipotent One.

XXVIII.—The Righteous Rise Again.

Righteousness and goodness, peace and true patience, and care concerning one's deeds, make to live after death. But a crafty mind, mischievous, perfidious, evil, destroys itself by degrees, and delays in a cruel death. O wicked man, hear now what thou gainest by thy evil deeds. Look on the judges of earth, who now in the body torture with terrible punishments; either chastisements are prepared for the deserving by the sword, or to weep in a long imprisonment. Dost thou, last of all, hope to laugh at the God of heaven and the Ruler of the sky, by whom all things were made? Thou ragest, thou art mad, and now thou takest away the name of God, from whom, moreover, thou shalt not escape; and He will award punishments according to your deeds. Now I would have you be cautious that thou come not to the burning of fire. Give thyself up at once to Christ, that goodness may attend thee.

XXIX.—To the Wicked and Unbelieving Rich Man.

Thou wilt, O rich man, by insatiably looking too much to all thy wealth, squander those things to which thou art still seeking to cling. Thou sayest, I do not hope when dead to live after such things as these. O ungrateful to the great God, who thus judgest thyself to be a god; to Him who, when thou knewest nothing of it, brought thee forth, and then nourished thee. He governs thy meadows; He, thy vineyards; He, thy herd of cattle; and He, whatever thou possessest. Nor dost thou give heed to these things; or thou, perchance, rulest all things. He who made the sky, and the earth, and the salt seas, decreed to give us back again ourselves in a golden age. And only if thou believest, thou livest in the secret of God. Learn God, O foolish man, who wishes thee to be immortal, that thou mayest give Him eternal thanks in thy struggle. His own law teaches thee; but since thou seekest to wander, thou disbelievest all things, and thence thou shalt go into hell. By and by thou givest up thy life; thou shalt be taken where it grieveth thee to be: there the spiritual punishment, which is eternal, is undergone; there are always wailings: nor dost thou absolutely die therein—there at length too late proclaiming the omnipotent God.

XXX.—Rich Men, Be Humble.

Learn, O thou who art about to die, to show thyself good to all. Why, in the midst of the people, makest thou thyself to be another *than thou art*? Thou goest where thou knowest not, and ignorantly thence thou departest. Thou managest wickedly with thy very body; thou thirstest always after riches. Thou exaltest thyself too much on high; and thou bearest pride, and dost not willingly look on the poor. Now ye do not even feed your parents themselves when placed under you. Ah, wretched men, let ordinary men flee far from you.

He lived, and I have destroyed him; the poor man cries out εὕρηκα. By and by thou shalt be driven with the furies of Charybdis, when thou thyself dost perish. Thus ye rich men are undisciplined, ye give a law to those, ye yourselves not being prepared. Strip thyself, O rich man turned away from God, of such evils, if assuredly, perchance, what thou hast seen done may aid thee. Be ye the attendant of God while ye have time. Even as the elm loves the vine, so love ye people of no account. Observe now, O barren one, the law which is terrible to the evil, and equally benignant to the good; be humble in prosperity. Take away, O rich men, hearts of fraud, and take up hearts of peace. And look upon your evil-doing. Do ye do good? I am here.

XXXI.—To Judges.

Consider the sayings of Solomon, all ye judges; in what way, with one word of his, he disparages you. How gifts and presents corrupt the judges, thence, thence follows the law. Ye always love givers; and when there shall be a cause, the unjust cause carries off the victory. Thus I am innocent; nor do I, a man of no account, accuse you, because Solomon openly raises the blasphemy. But your god is your belly, and rewards are your laws. Paul the apostle suggests this, I am not deceitful.

XXXII.—To Self-Pleasers.

If place or time is favorable, or the person has advanced, let there be a new judge. Why now art thou lifted up thence? Untaught, thou blasphemest Him of whose liberality thou livest. In such weakness thou dost not ever regard Him. Throughout advances and profits thou greedily presumest on fortune. There is no law to thee, nor dost thou discern thyself in prosperity. Although they may be counted of gold, let the strains of the pipe always be raving. If thou hast not adored the crucifixion of the Lord, thou hast perished. Both place and occasion and person are now given to thee, if, however, thou believest; but if not, thou shalt fear before Him. Bring thyself into obedience to Christ, and place thy neck under Him. To Him remains the honor and all the confidence of things. When the time flatters thee, be more cautious. Not foreseeing, as it behooves thee, the final awards of fate, thou art not able ever to live again without Christ.

XXXIII.—To the Gentiles.

O people, ferocious, without a shepherd, now at length wander not. For I also who admonish you was the same, ignorant, wandering. Now, therefore, take the likeness of your Lord. Raise upward your wild and roughened hearts. Enter steadfastly into the fold of your sylvan Shepherd, remaining safe from robbers under the royal roof. In the wood are wolves; therefore, take refuge in the cave. Thou warrest, thou art mad; nor dost thou behold where thou abidest. Believe in the one God, that when dead thou mayest live, and mayest rise in His kingdom, when there shall be the resurrection to the just.

XXXIV.—Moreover, to Ignorant Gentiles.

The unsubdued neck refuses to bear the yoke of labor. Then it delights to be satisfied with herbs in the rich plains. And still unwillingly is subdued the useful mare, and it is made to be less fierce when it is first brought into subjection. O people, O man, thou brother, do not be a brutal flock. Pluck thyself forth at length, and thyself withdraw thyself. Assuredly thou art not cattle, thou art not a beast, but thou art born a man. Do thou thyself wisely subdue thyself, and enter under arms. Thou who followest idols art nothing but the vanity of the age. Your trifling hearts destroy you when almost set free. There gold, garments, silver is brought to the elbows; there war is made; there love is sung of instead of psalms. Dost thou think it to be life, when thou playest or lookest forward to such things as these? Thou choosest, O ignorant one, things that are extinct; thou seekest golden things. Thence thou shalt not escape the plague, although thyself art divine. Thou seekest not that grace which God sent to be read of in the earth, but thus as a beast thou wanderest. The golden age before spoken of shall come to thee if thou believest, and again thou shalt begin to live always an immortal life. That also is permitted to know what thou wast before. Give thyself as a subject to God, who governs all things.

XXXV.—Of the Tree of Life and Death.

Adam was the first who fell, and that he might shun the precepts of God, Belial was his tempter by the lust of the palm tree. And he conferred on us also what he did, whether of good or of evil, as being the chief of all that was born from him; and thence we die by his means, as he himself, receding from the divine, became an outcast from the Word. We shall be immortal when six thousand years are accomplished. The tree of the apple being tasted, death has entered into the world. By this tree of death we are born to the life to come. On the tree depends the life that bears fruits—precepts. Now, therefore, pluck believingly the fruits of life. A law was given from the tree to be feared by the primitive man, whence comes death by the neglect of the law of the beginning. Now stretch forth your hand, and take of the tree of life. The excellent law of the Lord which follows has issued from the tree. The first law is lost; man eats whence he can, who adores the forbidden gods, the evil joys of life. Reject this partaking; it will suffice you to know what it should be. If you wish to live, surrender yourselves to the second law. Avoid the worship of temples, the oracles of demons; turn yourselves to Christ, and ye shall be associates with God. Holy is God's law, which teaches the dead to live. God alone has commanded us to offer to Him the hymn of praise. All of you shun absolutely the law of the devil.

XXXVI.—Of the Foolishness of the Cross.

I have spoken of the twofold sign whence death proceeded, and again I have said that thence life frequently proceeds; but the cross has become foolishness to an adulterous people. The awful King of eternity shadows forth *these things* by the cross, that they may now believe on Him. O fools, that live in death! Cain slew his younger brother by the invention of wickedness. Thence the sons of Enoch are said to be the race of Cain. Then the evil people increased in the world, which never transfers souls to God. To believe the cross came to be a dread, and they say that they live righteously. The first law was in the tree; and thence, too, the second. And thence the second law first of all overcame the terrible law with peace. Lifted up, they have rushed into vain prevarications. They are unwilling
to acknowledge the Lord pierced with nails; but when His judgment shall come, they will then discern Him. But the race of Abel already believes on a merciful Christ.

XXXVII.—The Fanatics Who Judaize.

What! art thou half a Jew? wilt thou be half profane? Whence thou shalt not when dead escape the judgment of Christ. Thou thyself blindly wanderest, and foolishly goest in among the blind. And thus the blind leadeth the blind into the ditch. Thou goest whither thou knowest not, and thence ignorantly withdrawest. Let them who are learning go to the learned, and let the learned depart. But thou goest to those from whom thou canst learn nothing. Thou goest forth before the doors, and thence also thou goest to the idols. Ask first of all what is commanded in the law. Let them tell thee if it be commanded to adore the gods; for they are ignored in respect of that which they are especially able to do. But because they are guilty of that very crime, they relate nothing concerning the commandments of God save what is marvelous. Then, however, they blindly lead you with them into the ditch. There are deaths too well known by them to relate, or because the heaping up of the plough closes up the field. The Almighty would not have them understand their King. Why such a wickedness? He Himself took refuge from those bloody men. He gave Himself to us by a superadded law. Thence now they lie concealed with us, deserted by their King. But if you think that in them there is hope, you are altogether in error if you worship God and heathen temples.

XXXVIII.—To the Jews.

Evil always, and recalcitrant, with a stiff neck ye wish not that ye should be overcome; thus ye will be heirs. Isaiah said that ye were of hardened heart. Ye look upon the law which Moses in wrath dashed to pieces; and the same Lord gave to him a second law. In that he placed his hope; but ye, half healed, reject it, and therefore ye shall not be worthy of the kingdom of heaven.

XXXIX.—Also to the Jews.

Look upon Leah, that was a type of the synagogue, which Jacob received as a sign, with eyes so weak; and yet he served again for the younger one beloved: a true mystery, and a type of our Church. Consider what was abundantly said of Rebecca from heaven; whence, imitating the alien, ye may believe in Christ. Thence come to Tamar and the offspring of twins. Look to Cain, the first tiller of the earth, and Abel the shepherd, who was an unspotted offerer in the ruin of his brother, and was slain by his brother. Thus therefore perceive, that the younger are approved by Christ.

XL.—Again to the Same.

There is not an unbelieving people such as yours. O evil men! in so many places, and so often rebuked by the law of those who cry aloud. And the lofty One despises your Sabbaths, and altogether rejects your universal monthly feasts according to law, that ye should not make to Him the commanded sacrifices; who told you to throw a stone for your offence. If any should not believe that He had perished by an unjust death, and that those who were beloved were saved by other laws, thence that life was suspended on the tree, and believe not on Him. God Himself is the life; He Himself was suspended for us. But ye with indurated heart insult Him.

XLI.—Of the Time of Antichrist.

Isaiah said: This is the man who moveth the world and so many kings, and under whom the land shall become desert. Hear ye how the prophet foretold concerning him. I have said nothing elaborately, but negligently. Then, doubtless, the world shall be finished when he shall appear. He himself shall divide the globe into three ruling powers, when, moreover, Nero shall be raised up from hell, Elias shall first come to seal the beloved ones; at which things the region of Africa and the northern nation, the whole earth on all sides, for seven years shall tremble. But Elias shall occupy the half of the time, Nero shall occupy half. Then the whore Babylon, being reduced to ashes, its embers shall thence advance to Jerusalem; and the Latin conqueror shall then say, I am Christ, whom ye always pray to; and, indeed, the original ones who were deceived combine to praise him. He does many wonders, since his is the false prophet. Especially that they may believe him, his image shall speak. The Almighty has given it power to appear such. The Jews, recapitulating Scriptures from him, exclaim at the same time to the Highest that they have been deceived.

XLII.—Of the Hidden and Holy People of the Almighty Christ, the Living God.

Let the hidden, the final, the holy people be longed for; and, indeed, let it be unknown by us where it abides, acting by nine of the tribes and a half...; and he has bidden to live by the former law. Now let us all live: the tradition of the law is new, as the law itself teaches, I point out to you more plainly. Two of the tribes and a half are left: wherefore is the half of the tribes *separated* from them? That they might be martyrs, when He should bring war on His elected ones into the world; or certainly the choir of the holy prophets would rise together upon the people who should impose a check upon them whom the obscene horses have slaughtered with kicking heel; nor would the band hurry rashly at any time to *the gift of* peace. Those of the tribes are withdrawn, and all the mysteries of Christ are fulfilled by them throughout the whole age. Moreover, they have arisen from the crime of two brothers, by whose auspices they have followed crime. Not undeservedly are these bloody ones thus scattered: they shall again assemble on behalf of the mysteries of Christ. But then the things told of in the law are hastening to their completion. The Almighty Christ descends to His elect, who have been darkened from our view for so long a time—they have become so many thousands—that is the true heavenly people. The son does not die before his father, then; nor do they feel pains in their bodies, nor polypus in their nostrils. They who cease depart in ripe years in their bed, fulfilling all the things of the law, and therefore they are protected. They are bidden to pass on the right side of their Lord; and when they have passed over as before, He dries up the river. Nor less does the Lord Himself also proceed with them. He has passed over to our side, they come with the King of heaven; and in their journey, what shall I speak of which God will bring to pass? Mountains subside before them, and fountains break forth. The creation rejoices to see the heavenly people. Here, however, they hasten to defend the captive matron. But the wicked king who possesses her, when he hears, flies into the parts of the north, and collects all *his followers.* Moreover, when the tyrant shall dash himself against the army of God, his soldiery are overthrown by the celestial terror; the false prophet himself is seized with the wicked one, by the decree of the Lord; they are handed over alive to Gehenna. From him chiefs and leaders are bidden to obey; then will the holy ones enter into the breasts of their ancient mother, that, moreover, they also may be refreshed whom he has evil persuaded. With various punishments he will torment those who trust in him; they come to the end, whereby offences are taken away from the world. The Lord will begin to give judgment by fire.

XLIII.—Of the End of This Age.

The trumpet gives the sign in heaven, the lion being taken away, and suddenly there is darkness with the din of heaven. The Lord casts down His eyes, so that the earth trembles. He cries out, so that all may hear throughout the world: Behold, long have I been silent while I bore your doings in such a time. They cry out together, complaining and groaning too late. They howl, they bewail; nor is there room found for the wicked. What shall the mother do for the sucking child, when she herself is burnt up? In the flame of fire the Lord will judge the wicked. But the fire shall not touch the just, but shall by all means lick them up. In one place they delay, but a part has wept at the judgment. Such will be the heat, that the stones themselves shall melt. The winds assemble into lightnings, the heavenly wrath rages; and wherever the wicked man fleeth, he is seized upon by this fire. There will be no succor nor ship of he sea. Amen flames on the nations, and the Medes and Parthians burn for a thousand years, as the hidden words of John declare. For then after a thousand years they are delivered over to Gehenna; and he whose work they were, with them are burnt up.

XLIV.—Of the First Resurrection.

From heaven will descend the city in the first resurrection; this is what we may tell of such a celestial fabric. We shall arise again to Him, who have been devoted to Him. And they shall be incorruptible, even already living without death. And neither will there be any grief nor any groaning in that city. They shall come also who overcame cruel martyrdom under Antichrist, and they themselves live for the whole time, and receive blessings because they have suffered evil things; and they themselves marrying, beget for a thousand years. There are prepared all the revenues of the earth, because the earth renewed without end pours forth abundantly. Therein are no rains; no cold comes into the golden camp. No sieges as now, nor rapines, nor does that city crave the light of a lamp. It shines from its Founder. Moreover, Him it obeys; in breadth 12,000 furlongs and length and depth. It levels its foundation in the earth, but it raises its head to heaven. In the city before the doors, moreover, sun and moon shall shine; he who is evil is hedged up in torment, for the sake of the nourishment of the righteous. But from the thousand years God will destroy all those evils.

XLV.—Of the Day of Judgment.

I add something, on account of unbelievers, of the day of judgment. Again, the fire of the Lord sent forth shall be appointed. The earth gives a true groan; then those who are making their journey in the last end, and then all unbelievers, *groan*. The whole of nature is converted in flame, which yet avoids the camp of His saints. The earth is burned up from its foundations, and the mountains melt. Of the sea nothing remains: it is overcome by the powerful fire. This sky perishes, and the stars and these things are changed. Another newness of sky and of everlasting earth is arranged. Thence they who deserve it are sent away in a second death, but the righteous are placed in inner dwelling-places.

XLVI.—To Catechumens.

In few words, I admonish all believers in Christ, who have forsaken idols, for your salvation. In the first times, if in any way thou fallest into error, still, when entreated, do thou leave all things for Christ; and since thou hast known God, be a recruit good and approved, and let virgin modesty dwell with thee in purity. Let the mind be watchful for good things.
Beware that thou fall not into former sins. In baptism the coarse dress of thy birth is washed. For if any sinful catechumen is marked with punishment, let him live in the signs *of Christianity*, although not without loss. The whole of the matter for thee is this, Do thou ever shun great sins.

XLVII.—To the Faithful.

I admonish the faithful not to hold their brethren in hatred. Hatreds are accounted impious by martyrs for the flame. The martyr is destroyed whose confession is of such kind; nor is it taught that the evil is expiated by the shedding of blood. A law is given to the unjust man that he may restrain himself. Thence he ought to be free from craft; so also oughtest thou. Twice dost thou sin against God, if thou extendest strifes to thy brother; whence thou shalt not avoid sin following thy former courses. Thou hast once been washed: shalt thou be able to be immersed again?

XLVIII.—O Faithful, Beware of Evil.

The birds are deceived, and the beasts of the woods in the woods, by those very charms by which their ruin is ever accomplished, and caves as well as food deceive them as they follow; and they know not how to shun evil, nor are they restrained by law. Law is given to man, and a doctrine of life to be chosen, from which he remembers that he may be able to live carefully, and recalls his own place, and takes away those things which belong to death. He severely condemns himself who forsakes rule; either bound with iron, or cast down from his degree; or deprived of life, he loses what he ought to enjoy. Warned by example, do not sin gravely; translated by the laver, rather have charity; flee far from the bait of the mousetrap, where there is death. Many are the martyrdoms which are made without shedding of blood. Not to desire other men's goods; to wish to have the benefit of martyrdom; to bridle the tongue, thou oughtest to make thyself humble; not willingly to use force, nor to return force used against thee, thou wilt be a patient mind, understand that thou art a martyr.

XLIX.—To Penitents.

Thou art become a penitent; pray night and day; yet from thy Mother *the Church* do not far depart, and the Highest will be able to be merciful to thee. The confession of thy fault shall not be in vain. Equally in thy state of accusation learn to weep manifestly. Then, if thou hast a wound, seek herbs and a physician; and yet in thy punishments thou shalt be able to mitigate thy sufferings. For I will even confess that I alone of you am here, and that terror must be foregone. I have myself felt the destruction; and therefore I warn those who are wounded to walk more cautiously, to put thy hair and thy beard in the dust of the earth, and to be clothed in sackcloth, and to entreat from the highest King will aid thee, that thou perish not perchance from among the people.

L.—Who Have Apostatized from God.

Moreover, when war is waged, or an enemy attacks, if one be able either to conquer or to be hidden, they are great trophies; but unhappy will he be who shall be taken by them. He loses country and king who has been unwilling to fight worthily for the truth, for his country, or for life. He ought to die rather than go under a barbarian king; and let him seek slavery who is willing to transfer himself to enemies without law. Then, if in warring thou shouldst die for thy king, thou hast conquered, or if thou hast given thy hands, thou hast perished uninjured by law. The enemy crosses the river; do thou hide under thy lurkingplace; or, if he can enter or not, do not linger. Everywhere make thyself safe, and thy friends also; thou hast conquered. And take watchful care lest anyone enter in that lurking-place. It will be an infamous thing if any one declares himself to the enemy. He who knows not how to conquer, and runs to deliver himself up, has weakly foregone praise for neither his own nor his country's good. Then he was unwilling to live, since life itself will perish. If any one is without God, or profane from the enemy, they are become as sounding brass, or deaf as adders: such men ought abundantly to pray or to hide themselves.

LI.—Of Infants.

The enemy has suddenly come flooding us over with war; and before they could flee, he has seized upon the helpless children. They cannot be reproached, although they are seen to be taken captive; nor, indeed, do I excuse them. Perhaps they have deserved it on account of the faults of their parents; therefore God has given them up. However, I exhort the adults that they run to arms, and that they should be born again, as it were, to their Mother from the womb. Let them avoid a law that is terrible, and always bloody, impious, intractable, living with the life of the beasts; for when another war by chance should be to be waged, he who should be able to conquer or even rightly to know how to beware.

LII.—Deserters.

For deserters are not called so as all of one kind. One is wicked, another partially withdraws; but yet true judgments are decreed for both. So Christ is fought against, even as Cæsar is obeyed. Seek the refuge of the king, if thou hast been a delinquent. Do thou implore of Him; do thou prostrate confess to Him: He will grant all things whose also are all our things. The camp being replaced, beware of sinning further; do not wander long as a soldier through caves of the wild beasts. Let it be sin to thee to cease from unmeasured doing.

LIII.—To the Soldiers of Christ.

When thou hast given thy name to the warfare, thou art held by a bridle. Therefore begin thou to put away thy former doings. Shun luxuries, since labor is threatening arms. With all thy virtue thou must obey the king's command, if thou wishest to attain the last times in gladness. He is a good soldier, always wait for things to be enjoyed. Be unwilling to flatter thyself; absolutely put away sloth, that thou mayest daily be ready for what is set before thee. Be careful beforehand; in the morning revisit the standards. When thou seest the war, take the nearest contest. This is the king's glory, to see the soldiery prepared. The king is present; desire that ye may fight beyond his hope. He makes ready gifts. He gladly looks for the victory, and assigns you to be a fit follower. Do thou be unwilling to spare thyself besides for Belial; be thou rather diligent, that he may give fame for your death.

LIV.—Of Fugitives.

The souls of those that are lost deservedly of themselves separate themselves. Begotten of him, they again recur to those things which are his. The root of Cain, the accursed seed, breaks forth and takes refuge in the servile nation under a barbarian king; and there the eternal flame will torment on the day decreed. The fugitive will wander vaguely without discipline, loosed from law to go about through the defiles of the ways. These, therefore, are such whom no penalty has restrained. If they will not live, they ought to be seen by the idols.

LV.—Of the Seed of the Tares.

Of the seed of the tares, who stand mingled in the Church. When the times of the harvest are filled up, the tares that have sprung up are separated from the fruit, because God had not sent them. The husbandman separates all those collected tares. The law is our field; whoever does good in it, assuredly the Ruler Himself will afford a true repose, for the tares are burned with fire. If, therefore, you think that under one they are delaying, you are wrong. I designate you as barren Christians; cursed was the fig-tree without fruit in the word of the Lord, and immediately it withered away. Ye do not works; ye prepare no gift for the treasury, and yet ye thus vainly think to deserve well of the Lord.

LVI.—To the Dissembler.

Dost thou dissemble with the law that was given with such public announcement, crying out in the heavenly word of so many prophets? If a prophet had only cried out to the clouds, the word of the Lord uttered by him would surely suffice. The law of the Lord proclaims itself into so many volumes of prophets; none of them excuses wickedness; thus even thou wishest from the heart to see good things; thou art also seeking to live by deceits. Why, then, has the law itself gone forth with so much pains? Thou abusest the commands of the Lord, and yet thou callest thyself His son. Thou art seen, if thou wilt be such without reason. I say, the Almighty seeks the meek to be His sons, those who are upright with a good heart, those who are devoted to the divine law; but ye know already where He has plunged the wicked.

LVII.—That Worldly Things are Absolutely to Be Avoided.

If certain teachers, while looking for your gifts or fearing your persons, relax individual things to you, not only do I not grieve, but I am compelled to speak the truth. Thou art going to vain shows with the crowd of the evil one, where Satan is at work in the circus with din. Thou persuadest thyself that everything that shall please thee is lawful. Thou art the offspring of the Highest, mingled with the sons of the devil. Dost thou wish to see the former things which thou hast renounced? Art thou again conversant with them? What shall the Anointed One profit thee? Or if it is permitted, on account of weakness, that thou foolishly profane...Love not the world, nor its contents. Such is God's word, and it seems good to thee. Thou observest man's command, and shunnest God's. Thou trustedst to the gift whereby the teachers shut up their mouths, that they may be silent, and not tell thee the divine commands; while I speak the truth, as thou art bound look to the Highest. Assign thyself as a follower to Him whose son thou wast. If thou seekest to live, being a believing man, as do the Gentiles, the joys of the world remove thee from the grace of Christ. With an undisciplined mind thou seekest what thou presumest to be easily lawful, both thy dear actors and their musical strains; nor carest thou that the offspring of such an one should babble follies. While thou thinkest that thou art enjoying life, thou art improvidently erring. The Highest commands, and thou shunnest His righteous precepts.

LVIII.—That the Christian Should Be Such.

When the Lord says that man should eat bread with groaning, here what art thou now doing, who desirest to live with joy? Thou seekest to rescind the judgment uttered by the highest God when He first formed man; thou wishest to abandon the curb of the law. If the Almighty God have bidden thee live with sweat, thou who art living in pleasure wilt already be a stranger to Him. The Scripture saith that the Lord was angry with the Jews. Their sons, refreshed with food, rose up to play. Now, therefore, why do we follow these circumcised men? In what respect they perished, we ought to beware; the greatest part of you, surrendered to luxuries, obey them. Thou transgressest the law in staining thyself with dyes: against thee the apostle cries out; yea, God cries out by him. Your dissoluteness, says he, in itself ruins you. Be, then, such as Christ wishes you to be, gentle, and in Him joyful, for in the world you are sad. Run, labor, sweat, fight with sadness. Hope comes with labor, and the palm is given to victory. If thou wishest to be refreshed, give help and encouragement to the martyr. Wait for the repose to come in the passage of death.

LIX.—To the Matrons of the Church of the Living God.

Thou wishest, O Christian woman, that the matrons should be as the ladies of the world. Thou surroundest thyself with gold, or with the modest silken garment. Thou givest the terror of the law from thy ears to the wind. Thou affectest vanity with all the pomp of the devil. Thou art adorned at the looking-glass with thy curled hair turned back from thy brow. And moreover, with evil purposes, thou puttest on false medicaments, on thy pure eyes the stibium, with painted beauty, or thou dyest thy hair that it may be always black.

The Instructions of Commodianus

God is the overlooker, who dives into each heart. But these things are not necessary for modest women. Pierce thy breast with chaste and modest feeling. The law of God bears witness that such laws fail from the heart which believes; to a wife approved of her husband, let it suffice that she is so, not by her dress, but by her good disposition. To put on clothes which the cold and the heat or too much sun demands, only that thou mayest be approved modest, and show forth the gifts of thy capacity among the people of God. Thou who wast formerly most illustrious, givest to thyself the guise of one who is contemptible. She who lay without life, was raised by the prayers of the widows. She deserved this, that she should
be raised from death, not by her costly dress, but by her gifts. Do ye, O good matrons, flee from the adornment of vanity; such attire is fitting for women who haunt the brothels. Overcome the evil one, O modest women of Christ. Show forth all your wealth in giving.

LX.—To the Same Again.

Hear my voice, thou who wishest to remain a Christian woman, in what way the blessed Paul commands you to be adorned. Isaiah, moreover, the teacher and author that spoke from heaven, for he detests those who follow the wickedness of the world, says: The daughters of Zion that are lifted up shall be brought low. It is not right in God that a faithful Christian woman should be adorned. Dost thou seek to go forth after the fashion of the Gentiles, O thou who art consecrated to God? God's heralds, crying aloud in the law, condemn such to be unrighteous women, who in such wise adorn themselves. Ye stain your hair; ye paint the opening of your eyes with black; ye lift up your pretty hair one by one on your painted brow; ye anoint your cheeks with some sort of ruddy color laid on; and, moreover, earrings hang down with very heavy weight. Ye bury your neck with necklaces; with gems and gold ye bind hands worthy of God with an evil presage. Why should I tell of your dresses, or of the whole pomp of the devil? Ye are rejecting the law when ye wish to please the world. Ye dance in your houses; instead of psalms, ye sing love songs. Thou, although thou mayest be chaste, dost not prove thyself so by following evil things. Christ therefore makes you, such as you are, equal with the Gentiles. Be pleasing to the hymned chorus, and to an appeased Christ with ardent love fervently offer your savor to Christ.

LXI.—In the Church to All the People of God.

I, brethren, am not righteous who am lifted up out of the filth, nor do I exalt myself; but I grieve for you, as seeing that out of so great a people, none is crowned in the contest; certainly, even if he does not himself fight, yet let him suggest encouragement to others. Ye rebuke calamity; O belly, stuff yourself out with luxury. The brother labors in arms with a world opposed to him; and dost thou, stuffed with wealth, neither fight, nor place thyself by his side when he is fighting? O fool, dost not thou perceive that one is warring on behalf of many? The whole Church is suspended on such a one if he conquers. Thou seest that thy brother is withheld, and that he fights with the enemy. Thou desirest peace in the camp, he outside rejects it. Be pitiful, that thou mayest be before all things saved. Neither dost thou fear the Lord, who cries aloud with such an utterance; even He who commands us to give food even to our enemies. Look forward to thy meals from that Tobias who always on every day shared them entirely with the poor man. Thou seekest to feed him, O fool, who feedeth thee again. Dost thou wish that he should prepare for me, who is setting before him his burial? The brother oppressed with want, nearly languishing away, cries out at the splendidly fed, and with distended belly. What sayest thou of the Lord's day? If he have not placed himself before, call forth a poor man from the crowd whom thou mayest take to thy dinner. In the tablets is your hope from a Christ refreshed.

LXII.—To Him Who Wishes for Martyrdom.

Since, O son, thou desirest martyrdom, hear. Be thou such as Abel was, or such as Isaac himself, or Stephen, who chose for himself on the way the righteous life. Thou indeed desirest that which is a matter suited for the blessed. First of all, overcome the evil one with thy good acts by living well; and when He thy King shall see thee, be thou secure. It is His own time, and we are living for both; so that if war fails, the martyrs shall go in peace. Many indeed err who say, With our blood we have overcome the wicked one; and if he remains, they are unwilling to overcome. He perishes by lying in wait, and the wicked thus feels it; but he that is lawful does not feel the punishments applied. With exclamation and with eagerness beat thy breast with thy fists. Even now, if thou hast conquered by good deeds, thou art a martyr in Him. Thou, therefore, who seekest to extol martyrdom with thy word, in peace clothe thyself with good deeds, and be secure.

LXIII.—The Daily War.

Thou seekest to wage war, O fool, as if wars were at peace. From the first formed day in the end you fight. Lust precipitates you, there is war; fight with it. Luxury persuades, neglect it; thou hast overcome the war. Be sparing of abundance of wine, lest by means of it thou shouldest go wrong. Restrain thy tongue from cursing, because with it thou adorest the Lord. Repress rage. Make thyself peaceable to all. Beware of trampling on thy inferiors when weighed down with miseries. Lend thyself as a protector only, and do no hurt. Lead yourselves in a righteous path, unstained by jealousy. In thy riches make thyself gentle to those that are of little account. Give of thy labor, clothe the naked. Thus shalt thou conquer.
Lay snares for no man, since thou servest God. Look to the beginning, whence the envious enemy has perished. I am not a

teacher, but the law itself teaches by its proclamation. Thou wearest such great words vainly, who in one moment seekest without labor to raise a martyrdom to Christ.

LXIV.—Of the Zeal of Concupiscence.

In desiring, thence thou perishest, whilst thou art burning with envy of thy neighbor. Thou extinguishest thyself, when thou inflamest thyself within. Thou art jealous, O envious man, of another who is struggling with evil, and desirest that thou mayest become equally the possessor of so much wealth. The law does not thus behold him when thou seekest to fall upon him. Depending on all things, thou livest in the lust of gain; and although thou art guilty to thyself, thou condemnest thyself by thy own judgment. The greedy survey of the eyes is never satisfied. Now, therefore, if thou mayest return and consider, lust is vain…whence God cries out, Thou fool, this night thou art summoned. Death rushes after thee. Whose, then, shall be those talents? By hiding the unrighteous gains in the concealed treasury, when the Lord shall supply to everyone his daily life. Let another accumulate; do thou seek to live well. And when thy heart is conscious of God, thou shalt be victor over all things; yet I do not say that thou shouldest boast thyself in public, when thou art watching for thy day by living without fraud. The bird perishes in the midst of food, or carelessly sticks fast in the bird-lime. Think that in thy simplicity thou hast much to beware of. Let others trangress these bounds. Do thou always look forward.

LXV.—They Who Give from Evil.

Why dost thou senselessly feign thyself good by the wound of another? Whence thou bestowest, another is daily weeping. Dost not thou believe that the Lord sees those things from heaven? The Highest says, He does not prove of the gifts of the wicked. Thou shalt break forth upon the wretched when thou shalt have gained a place. One gives gifts that he may make another of no account; or if thou hast lent on usury, taking twenty-four per cent, thou wishest to bestow charity that thou mayest purge thyself, as being evil, with that which is evil. The Almighty absolutely rejects such works as these. Thou hast given *that which has been* wrung from tears; that candidate, oppressed with ungrateful usuries, and become needy, deplores it. Besides having obtained an opportunity for the exactors, thy enemy for the present is the people; thou consecrated, hast become wicked for reward. Also thou wishest to atone for thyself by the gain of wages. O wicked one, thou deceivest thyself, but none else.

LXVI.—Of a Deceitful Peace.

The arranged time comes to our people; there is peace in the world; and, at the same time, ruin is weighing us down from the enticement of the world, (the destruction) of the reckless people whom ye have rent into schism. Either obey the law of the city, or depart from it. Ye behold the mote sticking in our eyes, and will not see the beam in your own. A treacherous peace is coming to you; persecution is rife; the wounds do not appear; and thus, without slaughter, ye are destroyed. War is waged in secret, because, in the midst of peace itself, scarcely one of you has behaved himself with caution. O badly fortified, and foretold for slaughter, ye praise a treacherous peace, a peace that is mischievous to you. Having become the soldiers of another than Christ, ye have perished.

I warn certain readers only to consider, and to give material to others by an example of life, to avoid strife, and to shun so many quarrels; to repress terror, and never to be proud; moreover, denounce the righteous obedience of wicked men. Make yourselves like to Christ your Master, O little ones. Be among the lilies of the field by your benefits; ye have become blessed when ye bear the edicts; ye are flowers in the congregation; ye are Christ's lanterns. Keep what ye are, and ye shall be able to tell it.

LXVIII.—To Ministers.

Exercise the mystery of Christ, O deacons, with purity; therefore, O ministers, do the commands of your Master; do not play the person of a righteous judge; strengthen your office by all things, as learned men, looking upwards, always devoted to the Supreme God. Render the faithful sacred ministries of the altar to God, prepared in divine matters to set an example; yourselves incline your head to the pastors, so shall it come to pass that ye may be approved of Christ.

LXIX.—To God's Shepherds.

A shepherd, if he shall have confessed, has doubled his conflict. Moreover, the apostle bids that such should be teachers. Let him be a patient ruler; let him know when he may relax the reins; let him terrify at first, and then anoint with honey; and let him first observe to do himself what he says. The shepherd who minds worldly things is esteemed in fault, against whose countenance thou mightest dare to say anything. Gehenna itself bubbles up in hell with rumors. Woe to the wretched people which wavers with doubtful brow! If such a shepherd shall be present to it, it is almost ruined. But a devout man restrains it, governing rightly. The swarms are rejoiced under suitable kings; in such there is hope, and the entire Church lives.

The Instructions of Commodianus

LXX.—I Speak to the Elder-Born.

The time demands that I alone should speak to you truth.

He is often admonished by one word which many refuse. I wish you to turn your hatred against me alone, that the hearts of all may tremble at the tempter. Look to the saying that truly begets hatred, (and consider) how many things I have lately indeed foretold concerning a delusive peace, while, alas, the enticing seducer has come upon you unawares, and because ye have not known how that his wiles were imminent, ye have perished; ye work absolutely bitter things, but that is itself the characteristic of the world; not any one for whom ye intercede acts for nothing. He who takes refuge from your fire, plunges in the whirlpool. Then the wretch, stripped naked, seeks assistance from you. The judges themselves shudder at your frauds…of a shorter title, I should not labor at so many lines. Ye who teach, look upon those to whom ye willingly tend, when for yourselves ye both receive banquets and feed upon them. For those things are ye already almost entering the foundations of the earth.

LXXI.—To Visit the Sick.

If thy brother should be weak—I speak of the poor man—do not empty-handed visit such an one as he lies ill. Do good under God; pay your obedience by your money. Thence he shall be restored; or if he should perish, let a poor man be refreshed, who has nothing wherewith to pay you, but the Founder and Author of the world on his behalf. Or if it should displease thee to go to the poor man, always hateful, send money, and something whence he may recover himself. And, similarly, if thy poor sister lies upon a sick-bed, let your matrons begin to bear her victuals. God Himself cries out, Break thy bread to the needy. There is no need to visit with words, but with benefits. It is wicked that thy brother should be sick through want of food. Satisfy him not with words. He needs meat and drink. Look upon such assuredly weakened, who are not able to act for themselves. Give to them at once. I pledge my word that fourfold shall be given you by God.

LXXII.—To the Poor in Health.

What can healthful poverty do, unless wealth be present? Assuredly, if thou hast the means, at once communicate also to thy brother. Be responsible to thyself for one, lest thou shouldst be said to be proud. I promise that thou shalt live more secure than the rich man. Receive into thy ears the teaching of the great Solomon: God hates the poor man to be a pleader on high. Therefore submit thyself, and give honor to Him that is powerful; for the soft speech—thou knowest the proverb—melts. One is conquered by service, even although there be an ancient anger. If the tongue be silent, thou hast found nothing better. If there should not wholesomely be an art whereby life may be governed, either give aid or direction by the command of Him that is mighty. Let it not shame or grieve you that a healthy man should have faith. In the treasury, besides, thou oughtest to give of thy labor, even as that widow whom the Anointed One preferred.

LXXIII.—That Sons are Not to Be Bewailed.

Although the death of sons leaves grief for the heart, yet it is not right either to go forth in black garments, or to bewail them. The Lord prudently says that ye must grieve with the mind, not with outward show, which is finished in the week. In the book of Solomon the promises of the Lord concerning the resurrection are forgotten if thou wouldest make thy sons martyrs, and thus with thy voice will bewail them. Art thou not ashamed without restraint to lament thy sons, like the Gentiles? Thou tearest thy face, thou beatest thy breast, thou takest off thy garments; and dost thou not fear the Lord, whose kingdom thou desirest to behold? Mourn as it is right, but do not do wrong on their behalf. Ye therefore are such. What less than Gentiles are ye? Ye do as the crowds that are descended from the diabolical stock. Ye cry that they are extinct. With what advantage, O false one, thou hast perished! The father has not led his son with grief to be slain at the altar, nor has the prophet mourned over a deceased son with grief, nor even has a weeping parent. But one devoted to God was hastily dying.

LXXIV.—Of Funeral Pomp.

Thou who seekest to be careful of the pomp of death art in error. As a servant of God, thou oughtest even in death to please Him. Alas that the lifeless body should be adorned in death! O true vanity, to desire honor for the dead! A mind enchained to the world; not even in death devoted to Christ. Thou knowest the proverbs. He wished to be carried through the forum. Thus ye, who are like to him, and living with untrained mind, wish to have a happy and blessed day at your death, that the people may come together, and that you may see praise with mourning. Thou dost not foresee whither thou mayest deserve to go when dead. Lo, they are following thee; and thou, perchance, art already burning, being driven to punishment. What will the pomp benefit the dead man? Thou shalt be accused, who seekest them on account of those gatherings. Thou desirest to live under idols. Thou deceivest thyself.

LXXV.—To the Clerks.

They will assemble together at Easter, that day of ours most blessed; and let them rejoice, who ask for divine entertainments. Let what is sufficient be expended upon them, wine and food. Look back at the source whence these things may be told on your behalf. Ye are wanting in a gift to Christ, in moderate expenditure. Since ye yourselves do it not, in what manner can ye persuade the righteousness of the law to such people, even once in the year? Thus often blasphemy suggests to many concerning you.

LXXVI.—Of Those Who Gossip, and of Silence.

When a thing appears to anybody of no consequence, and is not shunned, and it rushes forth, as if easy, whilst thou abusest it. Fables assist it when thou comest to pour out prayers, or to beat thy breast for thy daily sin. The trumpet of the heralds sounds forth, while the reader is reading, that the ears may be open, and thou rather impedest them. Thou art luxurious with thy lips, with which thou oughtest to groan. Shut up thy breast to evils, or loose them in thy breast. But since the possession of money gives barefacedness to the wealthy, thence every one perishes when they are most trusting to themselves. Thus, moreover, the women assemble, as if they would enter the bath. They press closely, and make of God's house as if it were a fair. Certainly the Lord frightened the house of prayer. The Lord's priest commanded with "sursum corda," when prayer was to be made, that your silence should be made. Thou answerest fluently, and moreover abstainest not from promises. He entreats the Highest on behalf of a devoted people, lest anyone should perish, and thou turnest thyself to fables. Thou mockest at him, or detractest from thy neighbor's reputation. Thou speakest in an undisciplined manner, as if God were absent—as if He who made all things neither hears nor sees.

LXXVII.—To the Drunkards.

I place no limit to a drunkard; but I prefer a beast. From those who are proud in drinking thou withdrawest in thine inner mind, holding the power of the ruler, O fool, among Cyclopes. Thence in the histories thou criest, While I am dead I drink not. Be it mine to drink the best things, and to be wise in heart. Rather give assistance (what more seekest thou to abuse?) to the lowest pauper, and ye shall both be refreshed. If thou doest such things, thou extinguishest Gehenna for thyself.

LXXVIII.—To the Pastors.

Thou who seekest to feed others, and hast prepared what thou couldest by assiduously feeding, hast done rightly. But still look after the poor man, who cannot feed thee again: then will thy table be approved by the one God. The Almighty has bidden such even especially to be fed. Consider, when thou feedest the sick, thou art also lending to the High One. In that thing the Lord has wished that you should stand before Him approved.

LXXIX.—To the Petitioners.

If thou desirest, when praying, to be heard from heaven, break the chains from the lurking-places of wickedness; or if, pitying the poor, thou prayest by thy benefits, doubt not but what thou shalt have asked may be given to the petitioner. Then truly, if void of benefits, thou adorest God, do not thus at all make thy prayers vainly.

LXXX.—The Name of the Man of Gaza.

Ye who are to be inhabitants of the heavens with God-Christ, hold fast the beginning, look at all things from heaven. Let simplicity, let meekness dwell in your body. Be not angry with thy devout brother without a cause, for ye shall receive whatever ye may have done from him. This has pleased Christ, that the dead should rise again, yea, with their bodies; and those, too, whom in this world the fire has burned, when six thousand years are completed, and the world has come to an end. The heaven in the meantime is changed with an altered course, for then the wicked are burnt up with divine fire. The creature with groaning burns with the anger of the highest God. Those who are more worthy, and who are begotten of an illustrious stem, and the men of nobility under the conquered Antichrist, according to God's command living again in the world for a thousand years, indeed, that they may serve the saints, and the High One, under a servile yoke, that they may bear victuals on their neck. Moreover, that they may be judged again when the reign is finished. They who make God of no account when the thousandth year is finished shall perish by fire, when they themselves shall speak to the mountains. All flesh in the monuments and tombs is restored according to its deed: they are plunged in hell; they bear their punishments in the world; they are shown to them, and they read the things transacted from heaven; the reward according to one's deeds in a perpetual tyranny. I cannot comprehend all things in a little treatise; the curiosity of the learned men shall find my name in this.

Elucidation.

I know nothing of the second poem of our author, and am indebted for the following particulars to Dr. Schaff.

It is an *apologetic poem* against Jews and Gentiles, written in uncouth hexameters, and discusses in forty-seven sections the doctrine concerning God and the Redeemer and mankind. It treats of the names of Son and Father; and here, probably, he lays himself open to the charge of Patripassian heresy. He passes to the obstacles encountered by the Gospel, warns the Jews and the Gentiles to forsake their unprofitable devotions, and enlarges on the eschatology, as he conceives of it. Let me now quote textually, as follows: —

"The most interesting part of the second poem is the conclusion. It contains a fuller description of Antichrist than the first poem. The author expects that the end of the world will come with the seventh persecution. The Goths will conquer Rome and redeem the Christians; but then Nero will appear as the heathen Antichrist, reconquer Rome, and rage against the Christians three years and a half. He will be conquered in turn by the Jewish and real Antichrist from the East, who, after the defeat of Nero and the burning of Rome, will return to Judea, perform false miracles, and be worshipped by the Jews. At last Christ appears, that is, God himself (from the *Monarchian* stand-point of the author) with the lost Twelve Tribes [?] as his army, which had lived beyond Persia in happy simplicity and virtue. Under astounding phenomena of nature he will conquer Antichrist and his host, convert all nations, and take possession of the holy city of Jerusalem."

This idea of a double Antichrist re-appears in Lactantius, *Inst. Div.*, vii. 16 seqq.

This second poem was discovered by Cardinal Pitra in 1852. The two poems were edited by E. Ludwig, Leipzig, 1877 and 1878.

www.ingramcontent.com/pod-product-compliance
Lightning Source LLC
Chambersburg PA
CBHW052043070526
44584CB00018B/2586